—THE—
GRAND OPENING

—OF THE—

U.S.A.
Speedway

WILL BE HELD IN

MAY=1917

Full Details will be Given in Ample
Time to Enable You to Make all
Necessary Arrangements.

Uniontown Speedway Association

"Official Program of the
Uniontown Speedway Association (U.S.A.)
Preliminary Thanksgiving Meet, 1916"

ISBN # 978-0-938833-29-1
Second Reprint 2009

Shore Publications, Copyright 2009

Shore Publications
P. O.Box 26
Chalk Hill, PA 15421
www.uniontownspeedway.com

Please also enjoy the 120 page vintage pictorial history book,
Yesteryear at the Uniontown Speedway
by Marci Lynn McGuinness.
Published by Shore Publications, Third Printing, 2009

Available at:
www.uniontownspeedway.com
All Shore Publications books at: www.ohiopyle.info.

Autographed copies of *Yesteryear at the Uniontown Speedway*:
Shore Publications, P. O. Box 26, Chalk Hill, PA 15421
$24.95 per copy plus tax and $5.50 shipping;

1916 Uniontown Speedway Program
$9.95, plus tax and $2.00 shipping

Add $1. per book for additional book shipping.

Contact for speaking engagements or wholesale orders:
shorepublications@yahoo.com or 724-437-2116

Publisher's Note...

The Uniontown Speedway Made History from the Start.
December 2, 1916
Frank Galvin Ran Over Hughie Hughes.
Galvin Hit the Press Stand Holding 100.
5 Died During this Preliminary Race.

Yesteryear at the Uniontown Speedway
by Marci Lynn McGuinness

1913 - 1915 Summit Mountain Hill Climbs
1916 - 1922 Uniontown Speedway boardtrack races
1940's Uniontown Speedway
Coal Baron Ball Team
1950's Uniontown Speedway
Mel Minnick, Sr. Profile

Notes...

George Titlow brought the first automobile to Uniontown in 1902.

In 1912, he organized the Fayette County Automobile Club.

In 1913, the first Summit Mountain Hill Climb was held.

In 1916, the Uniontown Speedway boardtrack was constructed.

In 1916, Universal Film Manufacturing Company's President, Carl Laemelle, donated the $3,000. solid silver Universal Trophy Cup.

www.uniontownspeedway.com

U. S. A. SPEEDWAY.

Constructed 1916.

Races under the rules and with the Sanction of the Contest Board of the American Automobile Association. Official Sanction No. 996.

PRELIMINARY OPENING,
THANKSGIVING MEET.
NOV. 30. 1916.

MANAGEMENT

President,
C. W. Johnson.

Secretary,
A. M. Hustead.

First Vice President,
Frank D. Saupp.

Treasurer,
Wendell A. Stone.

General Manager,
C. W. Johnson.

Asst. Gen. Manager,

OFFICIALS

Chairman Contest Board....Richard Kennerdell, New York
Representative Contest Board...F. H. Rosboro, Uniontown
Technical Committee Chairman..W. R. Strickland, Cleveland
Referee.........................Frank Rosboro, Uniontown
Starter.............................Webb Jay, Chicago
Assistant Starter..........Jno. L. Cadwalader, Pittsburgh
Director of Timing.............A. M. Crichton, Uniontown

U. S. A. SPEEDWAY.

Constructed 1916.

OFFICIALS (Continued)

Asst. Director of Timing . . . . Wallace Miller, Uniontown
Director of Scoring . . . . E. E. Porter, Uniontown
Clerk of Course . . . . Don. Beamer, Uniontown
Speed Reporter . . . . Homer Burchinal, Uniontown

JUDGES

John J. Bell and C. E. Jackson, of Pittsburgh.

SURGEONS

C. M. Luman,   E. H. Rebok,   A. S. Hagan,   Dr. Jackson

Technical Committee—John C. Donahue, Jos. Cronick,
Bert Abel.

Manager of Publicity . . . . . . Edw. F. Korbel, New York City
Manager of Events . . . . Neil Whalen, New York City
Chairman Press Board . . . . Geo. B. Smith, Uniontown
Scoreboard Manager . . . . W. R. Smith, Connellsville
Concession Committee—R. S. Cook, H. Keller, Amadee
Hagan, Zed Francis.

Manager of Pyrotechnics . . . . A. Bufano, Dunbar

Telegraph Service—Western Union and Postal Telegraph.

Telephone Service—Tri-State Telephone Co.

HUGHIE HUGHES

(HOSKINS SPECIAL)

Hughie Hughes is known as one of the best automobile drivers the world has ever seen. He is of the "old school" of which few are left today. Two continents have seen him at his best.

In 1904, in France, he drove a De Detrich car in the Gordon Bennett race. In 1911 he won the Savannah Trophy race in a Mercer,

1911 saw him third in the Grand Prize race in an Opn. Hughie won the Tacoma Potlatch contest in 1914, a Maxwell being his mount on this memorable occasion.

He has also won several hill-climbs with the Allen-Kingstons. Hughes took Walter Christie's front drive car and established a record of 110 miles an hour with it at the Indianapolis Speedway.

Hughie Hughes originated in England some thirty years ago and if he could get back today, he would in all probability show the Kaiser's sons some real speed either as a despatch bearer on terra firma, or as an aviator in His Majesty's service.

ARTHUR KLEIN
(CRAWFORD)

Arthur Klein heads the Crawford Team from Hagerstown, Md. He started in pursuit of racing fame about 1909, but first caught up with the elusive damsel when he began burning the bricks for the Indianapolis 500-mile race in 1911. He looked like a sure prize winner in that contest, but he went out with a broken valve stem when the race was about half over. Soon afterward, at Tacoma, Wash., he had better luck, finishing second in the Potlatch Trophy contest, and third in the Montamarathon. The latter race he probably would have won but for carburetor trouble and tire changes. Later Klein competed in races at Corona, San Diego, San Francisco and Venice, but in each of these races his car developed some weak spot he had previously overlooked. Klein then secured a new machine, which he named Klein-Art, after himself, and with which he has driven since.

Barney Newgard
(CRAWFORD)

Member of Crawford team. While not very well known in this vicinity, he has been following the racing game for some time. He had the position of head mechanic of the successful Dusenberg team. He later rode with Eddie O'Donnell until he met with his accident at Kansas City. He then joined the Devlin team with Hughie Hughes driving. Later he connected himself with the Crawford team under the management of Billy Chandler, riding with Art Klein.

This is his first mount, and his reputation for nerve and coolness will serve to keep him up among the leaders with the fast car he is driving.

FRANK GALVIN.
(PREMIER)
INDIANAPOLIS MOTOR SPEEDWAY ENTRY.

When most of our juveniles and ingenues of today were in short dresses, Frank Galvin was carving a name for himself as one of the greatest bicycle riders that ever straddled two wheels. He won the world's greatest pace following rider and won events for years in this country and Europe. He was equally good at sprinting and long distance work, winning several six-day races. When automobile racing superseded bicycle speed events, Galvin was not one of the first to take up the swifter game, the majority of the crack speed dare-devils having preceded him. But when Galvin did get in the game he was soon heard from and began to cause the other benzine jockies considerable worry on the speedway. He was here last summer for the hill climb, which was called off, and made many friends when he drove at the Youngwood meet.

Galvin first started driving racing cars in Europe, his first mount being a German Opel. His showing in this car was wonderful, considering that he was the only American on a foreign team. He attracted attention in this country first with the Buick "Bug" being unbeatable on dirt tracks. He then joined the famous Peugeot team, driving at Indianapolis and throughout the country. Through an accident he was out of racing a portion of the 1915 season. The Sunbeam was his next mount and he was in the money in every start, finishing the season with third place at Cincinnati in a field of 32 starters. At Chicago with the Premier he finished sixth and was second at New York in the Harkness trophy race, breaking all world's records for the distance, and averaging over 100 miles per hour. In this event he finished nine seconds behind his teammate Aitken, who won.

He will drive the Premier at Uniontown.

RALPH DE PALMA

Ralph De Palma has been for several years regarded among sporting experts generally, as the greatest all around driver the racing game has ever brought forth. In courage, resourcefulness and conservative driving, he is admitted to be without a peer. This is not only because of what he has accomplished, but because of the heady character of his work. His driving is distinguished by great steadiness and coolness, always calm and deliberate whether winning or losing. De Palma is of an exceptionally happy disposition. He is usually smiling, and there is a lilt of cheerfulness in his voice as he talks, so it is not surprising that he has thousands of friends and is a favorite with the "fans" wherever he starts in a contest.

De Palma shares with Harry Grant the distinction of being the only driver who captured the Vanderbilt Cup twice in succession. Ralph began driving racing automobiles in 1908 and probably has had the most meteoric career of any of the famous drivers. During his early racing days De Palma, although driving most brilliantly, was unlucky in road contests, but so successful was he in track events that he was crowned the "mile-track king."

In the 1908 Grand Prize at Savannah, De Palma drove three of the fastest laps, outdriving his American and European rivals, the latter including the great Nazzarro, Wagner, Hemery and Helm. While leading in this event, De Palma was forced out of the race nearing his last lap with a broken cylinder.

During his first year, Ralph won 10 firsts and 3 seconds out of 16 starts. In 1909, out of 47 starts he won 34 firsts, 8 seconds and 1 third—unplaced three times. The following year, out of 47 starts he won 30 firsts, 7 seconds and 3 thirds—unplaced three times. Since then he has won nearly 100 other contests on track, road and speedway, holding many speedway records for cars of 231-300 cubic inches. His latest important victory is the winning of the International 500-Mile Sweepstakes at Indianapolis, May, 1914, in which event he established a new record for the vitrified brick Hoosier course.

De Palma was born of Italian parentage, but he has called New York his home since early childhood.

THE TIMING OF BIG AUTOMOBILE RACES.

Unique System of Timing and Recording This Race Was Devised and Constructed by Local Men.

The system of timing races on the U. S. A. Speedway differs vastly from the system in vogue at other speedways, and the racing drivers are loud in their praise of it. In this unique system are incorporated the salient points of all other timing systems and the improved unique ideas of some of the brightest minds of the electrical and mechanical world. A great amount of credit is due A. M. Crichton, of the Tri-State Telephone Company, for the successful completion of the timing system. The cars mechanically register their own time in crossing the starting line. The number of laps made are electrically registered simultaneously at the timing table, the field scoreboard and the pit, thereby eliminating the possibility of an error in registering the number of laps made. The U. S. A. scoreboard is the only speedway where the number of laps is electrically registered. This same is true with reference to the registering of laps in th pits. The time made by the leading car and the rate of speed at which the car is running is posted on the big scoreboard every eighth lap. This serves to keep the audience thoroughly posted on the progress of the race.

WATCH THE BIG SCOREBOARD.

BERT WATSON.

(OLSEN)

A driver of Olsen car. Comes from New York. He made a reputation on dirt track, Brighton Beach. Has driven in all of the Sheepshead Bay speedway races, scoring places in three of them.

M. F. McBRIDE
Olsen.

Teammate of Bert Watson and a hard, clean-cut, conscientious worker. Nervy, cool and collected under all conditions. Popular with his fellow drivers, especially courteous in his treatment of his mechanician and assistants. His close attention to details has brought favorable comment on many occasions. While all cannot win, his popularity would cause no jealousy in the event of his being fortunate enough to finish first.

JOHN DE PALMA—J. J. R. Special.

Brother of Ralph De Palma of Indianapolis fame. Has driven in several events and is by no means a newcomer at the racing game. He was unfortunate with several of his early mounts and was unable to finish. He has been more fortunate of late and has made a very creditable showing in several races. He is driving a very fast car and expects to finish well up in the money. He drove the Universal Film Trophy car from New York to Uniontown.

JAMES A. BENEDICT—Benedict Special.

A resident of New York City, who drives for his love of the racing game. He is well and favorably known by motor enthusiasts of this vicinity, having attended the Summit Hill Climbing Contest of 1915. His experience on board speedways will be of vast service to him in this event. He finished fifth in the 100-mile Harkness Gold Trophy Race at Sheepshead Bay on October 28, and brings his car here in the pink of condition, and is full of confidence as to the result of the race. He says the home of the Universal Trophy is New York City.

DANGER PENNIES

How False Economy in Lubrication
Often Proves a Boomerang.

Mobiloils

A grade for each type of motor.

VACUUM OIL COMPANY
ROCHESTER, N. Y., U. S. A.

DAVE LEWIS.

(PREMIER)

INDIANAPOLIS MOTOR SPEEDWAY ENTRY.

Began driving dirt races in 1902. Prior to that he was amateur bicycle champion of California. He is the only California driver in the Uniontown races. He has won numerous sensational races. His first big racing showing being at Brighton Beach, New York. Four years ago at Brighton, in a series of races he won 20 out of 30 starts— a really remarkable performance considering the class of his competitors, which included the best men in the speed game. Among his victories are several at Ascot track, California, where he won races in 1914 and 1915. He holds the 100-mile beach record made at Old Orchard Beach, Maine. His first drives in big speedway races were as a member of the famous Stutz team, scoring places in a number of events. Lewis broke the world's five-mile record at Des Moines this season, time, 3 min. 2 sec., beating the former mark held by Caleb Bragg. The same day Lewis won in the 50-mile race at Des Moines. He also scored numerous second places this year—in the Chicago Grand Prix, the Tacoma Road Race, the Sioux City Speedway races, and the 50-mile race at Omaha. He may be looked upon as a strong contender at Uniontown.

OTTO HENNING
(OGREN)

Has been a race driver for six years. He was formerly with the Mercer team and was a racing partner of the late Spencer Wishart. The car he is driving has shown wonderful possibilities, and on the Chicago Speedway has shown continued speed of 105 miles per hour on the two-mile track. On the straightaway it has shown 115 miles per hour. Henning has driven in all the important major events this year and 1915. Ogren is the builder of both Ogren entries, and is a member of the S. A. E.

(FRONTENAC)

This veteran of the motor speed game is as famous as an automobile engineer as he is a driver. In 1908 he came to America and started out as Hemery's mechanician. When that driver went back to France, Chevrolet started on a barnstorming trip with a Buick. In 1909, in the Long Island trophy contest, he gained the distinction of being the first man to drive better than 70 miles an hour in a road race. While Chevrolet made a name for himself by breaking records and starting in every conceivable sort of a contest, he quit the game too early for many of the records to stand. Last year he brought his Delage to the Chicago Speedway, but for this race he is driving a Frontenac.

HAVE YOU TRIED

◯

Empire Tires

?

THEY WEAR LONGEST

◯

One Trial Convinces

HOW THE RACE IS RUN.

A Concise Account of How the Big Event is Managed.

SANCTION—The Thanksgiving Day race is run under the supervision of the American Automobile Association, the governing body of the sport. F. H. Rossgro, official representative of the Association, is in supreme control, with Webb Jay and A. M. Crichton as assistants in the roles of starter and chairman of timing. Minor appointments are made only with the sanction of these officials.

JUDGES—Order of the finish, in the event of a close race, is decided by the board of judges, while cases of unfair driving are passed on by umpires stationed at regular intervals about the course.

ELIGIBILITY—Before the start of the race, drivers are compelled to pass a medical examination certifying their physical fitness, and in other ways to give evidence of their capability. Their cars are also thoroughly inspected, to see that they do not exceed the standard of 300 cubic inches, and to establish proof that vital parts, such as the front axle, including all steering connections, have been replaced at least two days before the contest. The final touch is a brake test on the morning of the race. All these measures are designed to eliminate every possible chance of accident.

ELIMINATIONS—Only the 15 fastest cars can start the contest out of those entered, the remainder being eliminated in a series of time trials of one lap each held in the inverse order of entry. In the event of less than 15 cars being entered, a minimum of speed of eighty-five miles an hour is necessary to qualify.

START—The start is flying, all the contestants being paced around the course by Pres. C. W. Johnson, accompanied by Carl Laemmle, president of the Universal Film Company. When the starter's flag drops the first time around, the race is under way.

SCORING—The official score is kept by hand, no instrument having been invented as yet quite as reliable as the old-fashioned way, though ready information is given out through the medium of a special scoring machine consisting of thirty odometers with push buttons attached. This device makes it possible to arrive at lap and total standings instantaneously, for the especial benefit of the contestants.

ANNOUNCING—Information as to the progress of the race is transmitted to the spectators by means of announcers and scoreboards. There are more than 250 men engaged in this work. All scoreboards are constantly checked through a telephone system centering in the judges' stand, while announcing data is supplied through the Speedway press bureau, which covers every foot of the ground with a network of telephone wires.

SIGNALS—Signal flags generally used during the contest by the starter and his assistants are: Red, clear course; yellow, stop immediately; green, starting last lap; checkered, you are finished; white, stop for consultation, and blue, accident on course.

PRESS—Press accommodations at the Speedway are as ample as anywhere in the world, the main worker's stand accommodating 200 men, together with their telegraph operators, and the officials' paddock holding several hundred more. Information is furnished these men as quickly as it is available, thence to be distributed over myriads of trunk lines to all parts of the world. It is estimated no less than 25,000 publications will print the story of the contest the day afterward, with no less than 5,000 handling it in sport extras the day before.

POLICE—Provisions for safety of spectators are most complete, a thoroughly competent organization of guards handling every detail of the policing, together with numerous detectives and special officers. Cases of theft and fraud are comparatively rare, especially as spectators are constantly warned to be on their guard.

HOSPITAL—A complete hospital is maintained by the Speedway on the grounds, with every facility to take care of contestants, whether injured or overmaimed by the strain.

NEIL WHALEN.

Manager of Events.

Neil first drove at Lowell, Mass., in 1908, at the wheel of a Matheson car. A fly got in the carburetor and Neil lost time looking for flypaper to catch it and failed to win. Twenty-four racing next attracted him and he was seen in numerous "twice-around-the-clock grinds," finishing well up front in most cases. In October, 1909, he won the New York to Atlanta road race, covering 1063 miles in 54 hours 15 minutes. He drove the entire distance. He appeared at many dirt track meets and in 1910 won two of the 11 hill climbs he entered, losing to De Palma at Wilkes-Barre.

In 1912 Neil had one of the most spectacular smash-ups ever seen on a speedway, when he upset with a Case racer in the 500-mile race at Indianapolis, when an outside wheel came off. The car rolled over and over but neither driver or mechanic was hurt by the bumps and mashing.

Next season Neil will represent the U. S. A. Speedway at all of the big meets on the circuit, driving a new 145 h. p. racing car, now being constructed for him by Harry Miller, of Los Angeles. The car will be known as the "U. S. A. Special." In the meantime, he says, "Keep your eye on the new speedway. Thanksgiving Day the people of Uniontown will have something to be really-truly thankful for."

EAST LIBERTY TO UNIONTOWN

PITTSBURCH - E.LIBERTY
TO
U.S.A. SPEEDWAY
UNIONTOWN PENN.

Schedule of Pyrotechnics

9:00 A. M.—Salute.

9:30 A. M.—Bomb with 25 tickets for Grand Opening.

10:00 A. M.—Figured shell.

10:30 A. M.—Bomb with 25 tickets for Grand Opening.

11:00 A. M.—Salute.

11:30 A. M.—Bomb with 25 tickets for Grand Opening.

12:00 Noon —Figured shell.

One Mile Exhibition, Hughie Hughes, Sunbeam.

12:30 P. M.—Salute.

12:45 P. M.—Figured shell.

Five-Mile Exhibition, Hughie Hughes, Sunbeam.

1:00 P. M.—Salute. Brake test.

1:30 P. M.—Salute. Cars in position, drivers and mechanics in line for photo, parade and introduction of drivers.

1:50 P. M.—Salute, ten-minute signal.

2:00 P. M.—American flag with U. S. A. pennant and ticket bomb. Start of 100-lap races.

Figured shell.

Special exhibition, 10 miles, Sunbeam—Hughie Hughes driving in an attempt to lower world's record for 10 miles.

Figured shell. Cars in position for Event No. 2, 48 laps, 54 miles.

Flag bomb, start of Event No. 2.

Figured shell, races are over.

The above presents a vivid picture of the danger to driver and car on dirt tracks.

This is an actual photograph of a half-mile dirt track at Wilkes-Barre, Pa.

The driver on the right is John De Palma, brother of the famous Ralph, driving a Mercer car. The driver in the center is Neil Whalen, driving a National. The driver on the left is Harvey Ringland in a Mercer.

A careful study of the picture will show Whalen's car scraping the fence as he skids around the flat dirt track. The clouds of dust raised by the leading car make it almost impossible for the drivers in the rear to see either track or cars ahead. This condition does not exist on a board speedway similar in construction to the U. S. A. Speedway, and a speed of 100 miles per hour on a board track is less dangerous than a speed of 50 miles an hour on a flat dirt track.

Special Exhibition

Event No. 3—SPECIAL EXHIBITION TRIAL AGAINST TIME in an attempt to lower the American Speedway records at 1 mile, 5 miles, 10 miles.

Car.	Driver
SUNBEAM	HUGHIE HUGHES

LIST OF ENTRIES.

EVENT NO. 1—Class E. Non Stock. 300 cu. in. piston displacement, or under. Maximum weight 2500 pounds, 100 laps, 112½ miles.

FLYING START.

No.	Car	Driver	Mechanician
	Mercedes	Ralph De Palma	Louis Fountaine.
	Premier	Dave Lewis	J. McAllister.
	Premier	Frank Galvin	Gaston Weigle.
	Crawford	Barney Newgard	Emert N. Pala.
	Crawford	Arthur H. Klein	E. J. Longchamps.
	Hoskins	Hughie Hughes	
	J. J. R. Special	John De Palma	Billy Darragh.
	Benedict Special	Jas. A. Benedict	Frank J. Hanley.
	Olsen	M. P. McBride	Geo. Baldini.
	Olsen	Bert Watson	Wm. Claus.
	Adams Special		
	Pugh Special	James R. Meyer	Geo. Downs.
	Ogren Special	Otto Henning	
	Ogren Special	Hugh W. Ogren	
	Frontenac	Louis Chevrolet	R. C. Searles.
	Haynes	N. P. Fetterman	Burton Bailey.
	Haynes	H. L. Robinson	
	Haynes	Jack Conway	Geo. J. Halley.

LIST OF ENTRIES.

EVENT NO. 2—Class D. Non Stock. Free-for-All. For dealers residing within 150 miles of Uniontown, Pa.; 48 laps, 54 miles. Any dealer whose residence is within the above limit may enter in this event, one or more cars, of the same make he represents, providing the driver and mechanician also come within the residence qualification.

A dealer must be a representative of a factory marketing pleasure cars, and the cars entered must be of this manufacture. The car may be stripped and fitted with any gears, timed and tuned at the discretion of the dealer.

FLYING START.

No.	Car	Driver	Mechanician
	Murray Special	Fred McCarthy ...	Chas. McFarland.
	Packard Special	Wilmer Monahan ..	Brady Williams.
	Buick Special	Mike Hudoc	R. W. Patterson.
	Haynes Special	N. P. Fetterman ...	Burton Bailey.
	Haynes Special	J. F. Conway	Geo. J. Halley.
	Peerless Special	J. P. Fetterman	
	Buick Special	E. H. Willetts	Jos. Zimmel.
	Haynes Special	H. L. Robinson	
	National Special		
	Stearns Knight	C. S. Jones	F. M. Carthyor.
	Pathfinder		
	Crawford	Barney Newgard ..	Emert N. Pala.
	Crawford	Arthur Klein	E. J. Longchamps.
	Ford Special	Arthur Smith	R. S. Pastorius.

FROM THE MANAGEMENT.

OUR MAIDEN RACE.

We had hoped to have ready for your convenience and comfort at this meet, the entire Grandstand and reserved box accommodations, with a seating capacity of almost ten thousand, but we were doomed to disappointment and realize fully the meaning of Bobby Burns when he said: "The best laid plans of mice and men, gang aft aglee." Yet in the face of disappointment we are indeed gratified in being able in so short a space of time to throw open to the public the U. S. A. Speedway.

We have accomplished that which was deemed impossible in having completed the Speedway prior to Thanksgiving Day.

We have brought here for your entertainment, the world's racing stars. Men and mounts who hold numerous world's records. Men to whom fear is an unknown quantity and yet whose nerves have been tried in many prior contests. Men who could tell you of many harrowing moments when the fraction of a second determined life or death for them and the destruction of their cars. Men whose vocation demands clean living. Men who follow the straight and narrow path possibly more closely than the exponents of any other line of sports. Men whom it is a pleasure to mingle and associate with, whose education and intelligence is considerably above the average, many of whom are graduates of the leading colleges of this and other countries. The rapid development of the pleasure car is due entirely to the research and mechanical knowledge of the racing driver.

With the advent of spring, we will be able to beautify the Speedway grounds and provide many things for the comfort and convenience of our patrons.

We offer you an apology for the rough, unfinished condition of the stands, fences, roads and approaches, and want to assure you that on the occasion of our Grand Opening, in May, 1917, we will have the most beautiful, the most convenient and we hope the fastest Speedway in this country.

We crave your indulgence on this occasion. We thank you for your patronage and trust that we may have the pleasure of your company on many future occasions.

The Best Brand
After All

✦

WHIZ
Auto Specialties

THE BEST SELLER
BECAUSE
Quality Highest

—AT ALL—

Garages and
Supply Houses

C. W. JOHNSON

Promoter of the U. S. A. Speedway, President of Uniontown

Speedway Association.

To C. W. Johnson we concede the honor of bringing into existence the U. S. A. Speedway. This project was the creature of the brain of one of Fayette County's most progressive business men. For several years the racing bee buzzed in the ear of our worthy president. From boyhood days the desire to excel and lead in all manner of sports was prevalent in him, and his exuberant spirits found vent in participation in sporting events of all descriptions. His racing career dates back to the bicycle era, and his prowess on the bicycle is well known in this and adjoining counties.

His activities in Automobile Racing have been confined to road events. His memorable 20-hour run to Philadelphia and return is still fresh in the minds of Automobile enthusiasts, and the famous eleven-hour run to Baltimore and return stands out as an achievement of more than passing notice. The remarkable time in which he negotiated the Summit mountain in 1915, defeating such drivers as Ralph De Palma, and others equally as famous, in the remarkable time of 3 minutes and 27 seconds, stands out as an accomplishment hard to equal and harder still to excel. He is content to rest upon his laurels and enjoy the honors and rewards that come to a champion who retires undefeated.

Without his far-seeing eye, his resourceful brain and a tenacity of purpose great enough to overcome all obstacles, the U. S. A. Speedway would be a myth instead of a reality. To him and to him alone is due the honor, the praise and the glory of achieving that which even the most optimistic of us said "Could not be accomplished."

BOARD OF DIRECTORS.

JOHN S. PRINCE.

Designer and constructing engineer of the U. S. A. Speedway. Better known among the sporting fraternity as "Jack" Prince.

A short biography of the man who constructed the U. S. A. Speedway. In 1881, Jack was the champion cyclist of all Europe, holding the honor until 1884 when he came to America, where, in the city of Boston, he won the world's title, defeating all comers within his first two years here from San Francisco to the Massachusetts metropolis. In 1886 he settled in Omaha, put in races at the old Exposition building on Capitol Avenue, between the most noted professionals of this country—Shock, Knapp, Dingle, Eck Morgan, Marple, Reading and others. He built the old Coliseum, now the Ak-Sar-Ben, on 20th and Lake Streets, in 1887, and put in the best ten-lap bicycle track in the world of that time.

All the greatest riders on the globe were seen on this track at different times, as well as the star exponents of other sports and attractions. Prince had Adelina Patti and Nicolini in grand opera there, and he also had the famous Gilmore band at the Coliseum and all manner of big sporting events. The stupendous international tug-of-war, which will long be remembered by the old guard, was an event of his promotion, and it packed the old Coliseum for nine consecutive nights—nearly a quarter of a century ago. Jack also had Billy Muldoon, the champion wrestler, there, as well as Evan Lewis, the strangler; Tom Conners, Greener, McMillan, John L. Sullivan, Jack Dempsey, Charlie Mitchell, Jack Burke, the Irish Lad, all performing at the Coliseum under Prince's management. He had a skating rink, wolf chases, horses vs. bicycles, and all kinds of stirring amusements. He also got up the first exposition ever held in Omaha, and the historic old Coliseum was crowded to its capacity every night for two weeks.

OFFICIAL RECORDS.

SPEEDWAY RECORDS, REGARDLESS OF CLASS.

Distance	Time	Driver	Car	Place	Date
¼ Mile	8.16	Burman	Blitz'n Benz	Indianapolis	May 29, '11
½ Mile	16.80	Burman	Blitz'n Benz	Indianapolis	May 29, '11
1 Kilo	31.40	Burman	Blitz'n Benz	Indianapolis	May 29, '11
1 Mile	35.35	Burman	Blitz'n Benz	Indianapolis	May 29, '11
2 Mile	1:15.96	Bragg	Fiat	Los Angeles	Apr. 13, '10
3 Mile	1:54.82	Bragg	Fiat	Los Angeles	May 5, '12
4 Mile	2:33.37	Bragg	Fiat	Los Angeles	May 5, '12
5 Mile	3:11.75	Bragg	Fiat	Los Angeles	May 5, '12
10 Mile	6:35.62	Robertson	Simplex	Los Angeles	Apr. 9, '10
15 Mile	10:25.17	Hearne	Benz	Indianapolis	July 4, '10
20 Mile	12:58.14	Oldfield	Stutz	Indianapolis	May 30, '14
25 Mile	17:30.46	Oldfield	Stutz	Indianapolis	May 30, '14
50 Mile	33:45.32	Chriteans	Excelsior	Indianapolis	May 30, '14
75 Mile	50:21.24	Chriteans	Excelsior	Indianapolis	May 30, '14
100 Mile	1:10:46.50	Duray	Peugeot	Indianapolis	May 30, '14
150 Mile	1:46:20.00	Duray	Peugeot	Indianapolis	May 30, '14
200 Mile	2:25:11.00	Duray	Peugeot	Indianapolis	May 30, '14
250 Mile	3:00:58.48	Thomas	Delage	Indianapolis	May 30, '14
300 Mile	3:38:29.59	Thomas	Delage	Indianapolis	May 30, '14
350 Mile	4:15:22.69	Boillot	Peugeot	Indianapolis	May 30, '14
400 Mile	4:52:03.16	Thomas	Delage	Indianapolis	May 30, '14
450 Mile	5:37:33.50	Thomas	Delage	Indianapolis	May 30, '14
500 Mile	6:31:45.94	Thomas	Delage	Indianapolis	May 30, '14

CLASS "C" SPEEDWAY RECORDS.

(No Restrictions Other Than Piston Displacement).

160 Cubic Inches and Under.

Distance	Time	Driver	Car	Place	Date
5 Mile	4:26.08	Evans	Flanders	Indianapolis	Nov. 13, '11
10 Mile	8:53.97	Evans	Flanders	Indianapolis	Nov. 13, '11
15 Mile	13:24.00	Evans	Flanders	Indianapolis	Nov. 13, '11
20 Mile	17:54.83	Evans	Flanders	Indianapolis	Nov. 13, '11

161 to 230 Cubic Inches.

Distance	Time	Driver	Car	Place	Date
5 Mile	4:20.20	J. Nikrent	Buick	Los Angeles	Apr. 15, '10
10 Mile	8:40.17	J. Nikrent	Buick	Los Angeles	Apr. 15, '10
15 Mile	13:14.52	J. Nikrent	Buick	Los Angeles	Apr. 9, '10
20 Mile	17:37.36	J. Nikrent	Buick	Los Angeles	Apr. 9, '10
25 Mile	43:49.69	Tower	Flanders Spec	Los Angeles	May 5, '12
25 Mile	45:49.69	Endicott	Cole	Los Angeles	Apr. 9, '10

231 to 300 Cubic Inches.

Distance	Time	Driver	Car	Place	Date
1 Mile	45.60	De Palma	Mercer	Los Angeles	May 5, '12
2 Mile	1:31.53	De Palma	Mercer	Los Angeles	May 5, '12
3 Mile	2:17.17	De Palma	Mercer	Los Angeles	May 5, '12
4 Mile	3:02.70	De Palma	Mercer	Los Angeles	May 5, '12
5 Mile	3:47.34	De Palma	Mercer	Los Angeles	May 5, '12
10 Mile	7:27.93	De Palma	Mercer	Los Angeles	May 5, '12
15 Mile	11:11.17	De Palma	Mercer	Los Angeles	May 5, '12
20 Mile	14:56.65	De Palma	Mercer	Los Angeles	May 5, '12
25 Mile	18:53.20	J. Nikrent	Casw	Los Angeles	May 5, '12
50 Mile	42:35.08	Siefert	Dorris	Los Angeles	May 5, '12
75 Mile	1:03:54.28	Harroun	Marmon	Los Angeles	May 5, '12
100 Mile	1:25:22.07	Harroun	Marmon	Los Angeles	May 5, '12

SCORE AND POSITION OF CARS AT END OF 112½ MILES.

No.	Car	Driver	33 Laps		64 Laps		100 Laps		Mi. Per Hour
			Time	Pos	Time	Pos	Time	Pos	
	Mercedes	Ralph De Palma							
	Premier	Dave Lewis							
	Premier	Frank Galvin							
	Crawford	Barney Noward							
	Crawford	Arthur Klein							
	Hoskins	Hughie Hughes							
	J. J. R Special	John De Palma							
	Benedict Special	Jas. A. Benedict							
	Olsen	M. F. McBride							
	Olsen	Bert Watson							
	Adams Special								
	Pugh Special	James R. Meyer							
	Ogren Special	Otto Henning							
	Ogren Special	Hugh W. Ogren							
	Frontenac	Louis Chevrolet							
	Haynes	N. P. Fetterman							
	Haynes	H. L. Robinson							
	Haynes	Jack Conway							

SCORE AND POSITION OF CARS AT END OF 54 MILES.

No.	Car	Driver	16 Laps		32 Laps		48 Laps		Mi. Per
			Time	Pos.	Time	Pos.	Time	Pos.	Hour
	Murray Special	F. McCurdy							
	Packard Special	Wilber McMahon							
	Buick Special	Mike Hudoc							
	Haynes Special	N. P. Fetterman							
	Haynes Special	J. E. Conway							
	Peerless Special	I. P. Fetterman							
	Buick Special	E. H. Willets							
	Haynes Special	H. L. Robinson							
	National Special								
	Stearnes Knight	C. S. Jones							
	Pathfinder	A. Hughson							
	Crawford	Art Klein							
	Crawford	Barney Newbard							

IMPORTANT RULES GOVERNING RACE.

All automobile contests held in this country are conducted with the sanction and under the rules of the American Automobile Association. To a certain extent the same rules prevailing in road races govern contests on specially constructed courses, but the following may be cited as important speedway rules and will give a fair idea of what is expected of the contestants once the race is started:

The driver and mechanic of a car may be changed, if need be, during a race, but only at the end of a lap and upon application to the Referee. In case of disability or accident to the driver—but in no other case—the mechanic may replace him at any part of the course.

Should the mechanician leave his seat for any reason whatsoever at any time during the race, the driver must not continue until the mechanician is again seated in the car. In case of disability or accident to the mechanician which may necessitate his leaving the car, the driver may after stopping and investigating, proceed alone to the pits and make application to the Referee for instructions.

All mechanical repairs and adjustments must be made exclusively by the crew of a car. At the repair pits each contestant entering one car is entitled to have five attendants, including the team manager. For each additional car entered by the same contestant, he is entitled to three pit attendants. In other case only two pit attendants shall be permitted to make replacement of gasoline, oil and water and replacement or replenishment of tires, or crank the motor when contestant's car is at a standstill at the pits, but these attendants shall in no case make any mechanical repairs or adjustments to the car or assist in any manner in such repairs or adjustments.

Pit attendants are not allowed under any circumstances to pump air or oil into the car.

Spare parts, tools, etc., may be laid on the shelf or ledge in front of the pit, and pit attendants, while in the pit, but not otherwise, may hand same to the driver or mechanic. No car is permitted to leave its pit until all tools, tires, etc., on the ground in front of the pit shall have been removed.

All renewals of fuel, oil, water and replenishments of damaged parts have to be made at the repair pits at the start and finish line, except in case of emergency. Where a car is disabled on the track and cannot proceed under its own power to the pits, the crew of the car may report to the Referee, who, in his discretion may allow the crew to obtain necessary fuel and parts (except tires) as will enable the car to proceed under its own power. Such replenishments or replacements must be made by the crew unassisted.

Tires may be taken on at the pits, and, if necessary, at any section of the course, provided in the latter case that extra tires are carried on the car. Any competing car voluntarily leaving the course will be disqualified.

IMPORTANT RULES GOVERNING THE RACE.

Event No. 2

Any dealer whose residence is within the above limit, may enter in this event, one or more cars, of the same make he represents, providing the driver and mechanician also come within the residence qualification.

A dealer must be a representative of a factory marketing pleasure cars and the cars entered must be of this manufacture. The car can be stripped and fitted with any gears, timed and tuned at the discretion of the dealer.

In addition to the general rules and conditions, note carefully the following approved special conditions which will apply to the Dealers' Race:

1st—All tires must be fastened on the rims with 12 lugs exclusive of valve lugs.

2nd—If more than fifteen cars qualify, the following conditions will finally determine the starters:

(a) The individual car of the make which is represented by the largest number of entries, making the best time in the official speed trials, will be awarded first starting position. The individual car of the make represented by the next largest number of entries making the best time in the official speed trials will be awarded second starting position. Succeeding positions will be awarded in the same manner until the fastest cars of each make which is represented by more than one qualified entry shall have been placed.

(b) The fastest cars representing makes of which only one car has qualified will then be given the next open starting positions in order.

(c) If the methods outlined in the paragraphs do not fill fifteen positions, the starters in the remaining positions will be determined by a special five-lap race, open only to the remaining cars which have qualified in the official speed trials, but have been eliminated by the above conditions, to be held on the last day of the qualifying trials (November 29th), and the order of finish of the necessary number of cars in this event will govern, except that under no conditions may more than three cars of any one make start.

Hagan's
Ice Cream

"A STANDARD OF EXCELLENCE"

I. N. HAGAN ICE CREAM CO.

UNIONTOWN, PENNA.

PRIZES TO BE AWARDED.

Cash Prizes Totaling $4,250.00.

EVENT No. 1. Class E. Non Stock; 300 Cubic Inches Piston Displacement or Under.

MAXIMUM WEIGHT, 2,500 Pounds, 100 Laps, 112½ Miles.

FIRST PRIZE	$1000.00
SECOND PRIZE	700.00
THIRD PRIZE	500.00
FOURTH PRIZE	400.00
FIFTH PRIZE	300.00
FOR CAR LEADING AT 45 LAPS	100.00
A TOTAL OF	$3000.00

EVENT No. 2. Class D. Non Stock. FREE-FOR-ALL; 48 Laps, 54 Miles.

FOR DEALERS RESIDING WITHIN 150 MILES OF UNIONTOWN.

FIRST PRIZE	$ 500.00
SECOND PRIZE	300.00
THIRD PRIZE	200.00
FOURTH PRIZE	100.00
FIFTH PRIZE	50.00
AND	50.00

Extra to car making fastest time for both 16 and 32 laps.

A TOTAL OF	$1250.00

Universal Film Trophy, valued at $3000.00, Awarded to the Winner of Event No. 1.

SIGNALLING TO CONTESTANTS.

An important feature of an automobile contest, particularly one held on a specially constructed course where speeds of 90 to 100 miles an hour are being made, is the method of keeping the contestants in touch with the officials of the race. In the early days of competition a system of flag signalling was devised and is now used in all automobile races throughout the world. This system, known as the International Road Racing Signals, is entirely under the control of the starter, and consists of a series of colored flags having the following meanings:

RED—Course is clear.

YELLOW—Blocked course; stop.

GREEN—You are entering your last lap.

WHITE—Stop at pits on next lap for consultation.

BLACK AND WHITE CHECKERED—You are finished.

BLACK WITH WHITE CENTER—A competitor is trying to overtake you. (Used only in road races.)

THE NATIONAL PIKE.

The National Pike, nearly a century old, is still one of the most magnificent roadways in the world and every foot of its course through the mountains appeals to the sense of the romantic and beautiful in nature.

This famous road was the outgrowth of the pressing need, a hundred years ago, for better means of travel than then existed between the eastern and western sections of the country. It was in 1806 that a commission was appointed to lay out the road and the money to cover the expense was voted by Congress. A road owned by individuals was at this time in use between Baltimore and Cumberland, and the National Road as laid out by this Commission, was to connect with this road at Cumberland and continue west; the two together to constitute the National Pike. The road was completed and opened to the public in 1818. It was intended that this road starting in Baltimore, would reach to St. Louis, Mo. It was, however, only completed a short distance west of Indianapolis, Ind.

The part of the National Pike between Uniontown, Pa., and Cumberland, Md., passes through a section rich in historical interest. It crosses and follows in places the course of the road opened for Braddock's army in 1754, which road largely followed the Indian trail, known as the Nemacolin Path. After the close of the French and Indian War, the military road was re-opened and until 1812 was known as Braddock's Road. (At the Summit of Chestnut Ridge, three miles east from the Speedway, a road runs to the north one mile from the Pike to Washington's Springs, where the Half King was encamped when the presence of Jumonville's party in the vicinity was discovered. Farther along this road passes near the scene of Washington's attack upon Jumonville, May 28, 1754, and Jumonville's grave.)

A little over six miles east from the Speedway to the north of the road, is Braddock's grave, at present marked by a tablet erected by the Fayette County Historical Society. About fifty acres of the ground surrounding it has been purchased by private subscription, to be known as Braddock Park. This has been enclosed by a fence and the grounds improved by shrubbery and driveways, and a monument typifying Braddock's services to this country will be erected near the grave.

A little over a mile farther east on the Pike, is Mount Washington. At present a large brick house stands on the south side of the road and a lane leads from the yard down to the valley where the site of old Fort Necessity is still visible from the Pike. It was here that Washington suffered his only defeat in battle, that with the French and Indians.

Somerfield, where the counties of Fayette and Somerset are connected by a stone bridge, built over the Youghiogheny River in 1818, was formerly known as Big Crossings and identified with many historical events prior to and after the French and Indian War. In crossing, notice the tablet lately erected by Historical Society on the north side of the bridge.

There are many other places of historical interest between the Speedway and Hagerstown. For a long time this road was sadly neglected, but during the past three or four years the State Road Departments of both Pennsylvania and Maryland have been expending large sums of money to put it in first class condition. Bridges have all been rebuilt, breakers are taken out in Pennsylvania, and mostly levelled down in Maryland. We now have an improved highway from the Speedway to the Atlantic Coast. It has the easiest grades and most beautiful scenery of any of the east and west roads over the mountains in Pennsylvania or Maryland.

HUDSON
SUPER
SIX

EDDIE BALD MOTOR CAR CO., DISTRIBUTORS,

5860 Baum Boulevard,

PITTSBURGH,   PENNA.

E. F. Korbel

In Charge of the Publicity of the U. S. A. Speedway.

Messrs. Colwell and Korbel are New York's leading publicity promoters and have directed the publicity of many of the biggest automobile races and expositions of various sorts throughout the country.

M. W. COLWELL

History of the U. S. A. Speedway

The construction of the U. S. A. planked speedway will go down in the annals of history as an accomplishment which a retrospective view shows has never been equaled.

The construction of board speedways, by reason of the many millions of feet of lumber used and the special quality and grade required, is under ordinary circumstances necessarily slow and tedious. The average time required to fill an order of such magnitude as the order for lumber used in this speedway, is ordinarily six months, and under such extraordinary market conditions as at present exist it is extremely hard to place such an order with any assurance of its being filled under nine months, and even on such datings, only the very large manufacturers will accept such an order.

Had it not been for the enormous manufacturing facilities of the American Lumber Company of Pittsburgh, Pa., and the personal interest taken in this project by one of the members of the firm, it would have been an utter impossibility to have brought this matter to a conclusion in such a short space of time.

The signing of the ground leases was attested on August 22, 1916. Just three months ago the present site of the Speedway was a verdant meadow, where the cows chewed their cuds in contentment, and sheep and lambs and horses and colts roamed over its broad acres. What a change in so short a space of time. The roar and bark of the racing automobile is a strange contrast to the peaceful scene of less than three months ago.

The order for the lumber was placed with the American Lumber Co. on September 8, 1916.

The first lumber was delivered on the grounds September 15.

The first survey was made August 21.

The first stake was driven September 1.

The first supporting timber was raised September 18.

The first surface plank was laid November 1.

The erection of the boxes was started November 24.

The surface of the track was completed November 25.

The first racing car was admitted to the track November 21. It was a Crawford, driven by Barney Newgard.

And now on this, Thanksgiving Day, we render thanks to all those who have lent their assistance in the completion of the U. S. A. Speedway and have made possible this day of pleasure for thousands of people.

UNIONTOWN SPEEDWAY ASSOCIATION.

GRAND STANDS AND GENERAL ADMISSION GATES

Hotel Keepers' Association

OF UNIONTOWN, PA.

(Continued on Next Page.)

List of Uniontown Hotels

James Moran	Central Hotel	John W. Lee	McClellan
R. W. Beall	Brunswick Hotel	William Farnsworth	Altman Hotel
Bert Rush	West End Hotel	Walter Lazier, M'g'r.	Duquesne Hotel
John F. Reagan	Lafayette Hotel	R. F. Sample	The Gallatin
Geo. W. Wilkinson	Hotel Exchange	George F. Titlow	Hotel Titlow

Geo. W. Wilkinson, President.   R. F. Sample, Secy.

MEMORANDUM

TABLE OF CONTENTS.

INDEX TO ADVERTISEMENTS.

I. P. FETTERMAN

"Red," as he is more favorably known, needs no introduction to motor enthusiasts of this and adjoining counties. He finished second in the Summit Hill Climb of 1915, and his daring and remarkable driving in that race elicited a great deal of favorable comment. He has participated in quite a number of races on dirt tracks, and piloted home several winners. The beautiful car he is piloting in this race is the entry of the Hiland Automobile Co. of Pittsburgh. "Red" expects to finish well up among the leaders.

WILMER MONAHAN
(PACKARD)

Better known as "Monnie," who will pilot the Packard "Greyhound," owned by the Standard Garage of Uniontown. Monahan is noted for his daring and fearless driving. During the season of 1915 he piloted several mounts in adjoining counties on dirt tracks and made an enviable record. This is his first race on a board speedway.

PAY NO MORE

THAN PRICES GIVEN BELOW

LIST OF REFRESHMENTS
Sold on Speedway Grounds

Cracker Jack 5c	Weinie Sandwich 10c
Salted Peanuts, Pkg.... 5c	Bread Ham Sandwich ..20c
Jumbo Peanuts, Pkg. ... 5c	Cheese Sandwich 10c
Pop 5c	Minced Ham 10c
Ice Cream Cones 10c	Hot Coffee 10c
Cigars 10c	Buttermilk 5c
Cigars ... .15c	National Biscuits 15c
Cigars, Two for ,......25c	Chicken Sandwich 25c
Imported Cigars, St't...25c	Box Lunch 25c
Cigarettes 10c	Lunch Loaf 20c
Cigarettes 25c	Box Lunch 50c
Cigarettes ... .35c	Chicken Box Lunch ..$1.00
Small Pkg. Candy, 5c & 10c	Half-Lb. Box Candy ...35c

These Prices Are Standard Throughout Grounds

DO NOT PAY MORE.

MIKE HUDOC

(BUICK)

A resident of Uniontown who will pilot the Buick "Yellow Kid" owned by the Standard Garage of Uniontown. A quiet, conservative, and yet jovial boy, who is very popular with the drivers of this vicinity. His former activities have been confined to dirt tracks, upon which he has piloted many winning mounts. With the speed that the "Yellow Kid" is known to possess, he expects to make a creditable showing in his first race on a board speedway.

Compliments of

Keller's Soda Works

Resta Always Rides on Silvertowns.

Why Don't You Ride On

GOODRICH

SILVERTOWN

CABLE-CORD TIRES?

You've seen the performance of this wonderful tire.
You know that practically all the great racers use nothing
else. And that they require fewest changes through the
gruelling runs. Why not enjoy their wonderful **Durability**?

SPEED and FUEL SAVING!

Think What These Tremendous Silvertown Advantages
Would Mean in Every Day Use on YOUR Car!

Patented and Made Only by

THE B. F. GOODRICH COMPANY

Factories,
Akron, O.

Branches and
Dealers Everywhere.

FRED McCARTHY

Murray Special.

Entry of the Murray Motor Car Co.

A very popular boy among the professional racing drivers. For several years he acted as mechanician for Dario Resta and the world famous champion of the present racing season is loud in his praise of the nervy, courageous driver of the Murray Special. The Murray Motor Car Co. is to be congratulated on its selection of such a capable driver. The Murray Special is one of the most beautiful cars to participate in this meet.

N. P. FETTERMAN

Haynes Special.

Brother of the popular "Red" Fetterman. While this is his first race on a board speedway, yet his former experience, covering a period of four years, amply qualifies him for a mount in this race. His car is fast and will undoubtedly make a creditable showing. He is one of the most popular drivers of the Pittsburgh district.

HOUR RECORDS
U. S. A. Speedway

When a Car is Traveling at Rate of	It's Making a Lap in
120 Miles Per Hour	33.75 Seconds
119 Miles Per Hour	34.03 Seconds
118 Miles Per Hour	34.31 Seconds
117 Miles Per Hour	34.61 Seconds
116 Miles Per Hour	34.91 Seconds
115 Miles Per Hour	35.21 Seconds
114 Miles Per Hour	35.51 Seconds
113 Miles Per Hour	35.84 Seconds
112 Miles Per Hour	36.16 Seconds
111 Miles Per Hour	36.48 Seconds
110 Miles Per Hour	36.82 Seconds
109 Miles Per Hour	37.16 Seconds
108 Miles Per Hour	37.50 Seconds
107 Miles Per Hour	37.85 Seconds
106 Miles Per Hour	38.22 Seconds
105 Miles Per Hour	38.57 Seconds
104 Miles Per Hour	38.94 Seconds
103 Miles Per Hour	39.32 Seconds
102 Miles Per Hour	39.70 Seconds
101 Miles Per Hour	40.10 Seconds
100 Miles Per Hour	40.50 Seconds
99 Miles Per Hour	40.91 Seconds
98 Miles Per Hour	41.32 Seconds
97 Miles Per Hour	41.75 Seconds
96 Miles Per Hour	42.19 Seconds
95 Miles Per Hour	42.63 Seconds
94 Miles Per Hour	43.08 Seconds
93 Miles Per Hour	43.54 Seconds
92 Miles Per Hour	44.02 Seconds
91 Miles Per Hour	44.50 Seconds
90 Miles Per Hour	45.00 Seconds
89 Miles Per Hour	45.50 Seconds
88 Miles Per Hour	46.02 Seconds
87 Miles Per Hour	46.55 Seconds
86 Miles Per Hour	47.09 Seconds
85 Miles Per Hour	47.65 Seconds
84 Miles Per Hour	48.21 Seconds
83 Miles Per Hour	48.79 Seconds
82 Miles Per Hour	49.39 Seconds
81 Miles Per Hour	50.00 Seconds
80 Miles Per Hour	50.63 Seconds
79 Miles Per Hour	51.27 Seconds
78 Miles Per Hour	51.92 Seconds
77 Miles Per Hour	52.60 Seconds
76 Miles Per Hour	53.28 Seconds
75 Miles Per Hour	54.00 Seconds

"GOING SOME"

The Citizens Title and Trust Company

Uniontown, Pa.

Statement of Condition at Close of Business, Nov. 24th, Nineteen Hundred Sixteen.

RESOURCES.

Loans and Investments	$1,508,273.80
Banking House, Real Estate Investments & etc.	277,192.44
Miscellaneous	7,778.62
Cash and Due from Banks	697,702.66
Trust Investments and Cash	497,363.19
	$2,988,310.71

LIABILITIES.

Capital Stock	$ 150,000.00
Surplus and Undivided Profits	312,150.47
Interest not Credited	9,676.67
Deposits	2,012,446.38
Miscellaneous	6,674.00
Due Trust Estates	497,363.19
	$2,988,310.71

Resources March 30th, 1916	$2,488,275.36
Resources November 17th, 1916	2,840,250.51
RESOURCES NOVEMBER 24, 1916	$2,988,310.71

A Progressive Institution.

FAYETTE COUNTY'S

LEADING BEER

LABOR

Labor Brewing Co.

UNIONTOWN, PA.

STANDARD GARAGE

C. W. Johnson, Owner

UNIONTOWN   PENNA.